KT-513-461

FIFE EDUCATION
COMMITTEE

KING'S ROAD P. SCHOOL
ROSYTH

KT-513-461

PASSPORT TO

# GREAT BRITAIN

Andrew Langley

## Franklin Watts

London/New York/Sydney/Toronto

Copyright © 1985 Franklin Watts Limited

First published in Great Britain by
Franklin Watts Limited
12a Golden Square
London W1R 4BA

First published in the USA by
Franklin Watts Inc.
387 Park Avenue South
New York
N.Y. 10016

First published in Australia by
Franklin Watts Australia
14 Mars Road
Lane Cove
NSW 2066

UK ISBN: 0 86313 288 X
US ISBN: 0-531-10015-4
Library of Congress Catalog Card No: 85-50171

Design: Edward Kinsey
        Cooper-West
Illustrations: Hayward Art Group
Consultant: Keith Lye

Photographs: Chris Fairclough, Zefa, J. Allan
Cash, Scottish Tourist Board, Aerofilms, Tesco,
Coloursport, Granada Television, BBC Copyright
Photograph, Franklin Watts Picture Library,
National Dairy Council, National Coal Board,
Shell Petroleum, British Leyland, Plessey, British
Aerospace, British Railways, National Portrait
Gallery, Tate Gallery, The Mansell Collection,
Popperfoto, Camera Press, Associated Press, Reflex

Front cover: Zefa, National Coal Board, Plessey,
Chris Fairclough
Back cover: Zefa

Phototypeset by Keyspools Limited
Colour reproductions by Hongkong Graphic Arts
Printed in Belgium

# Contents

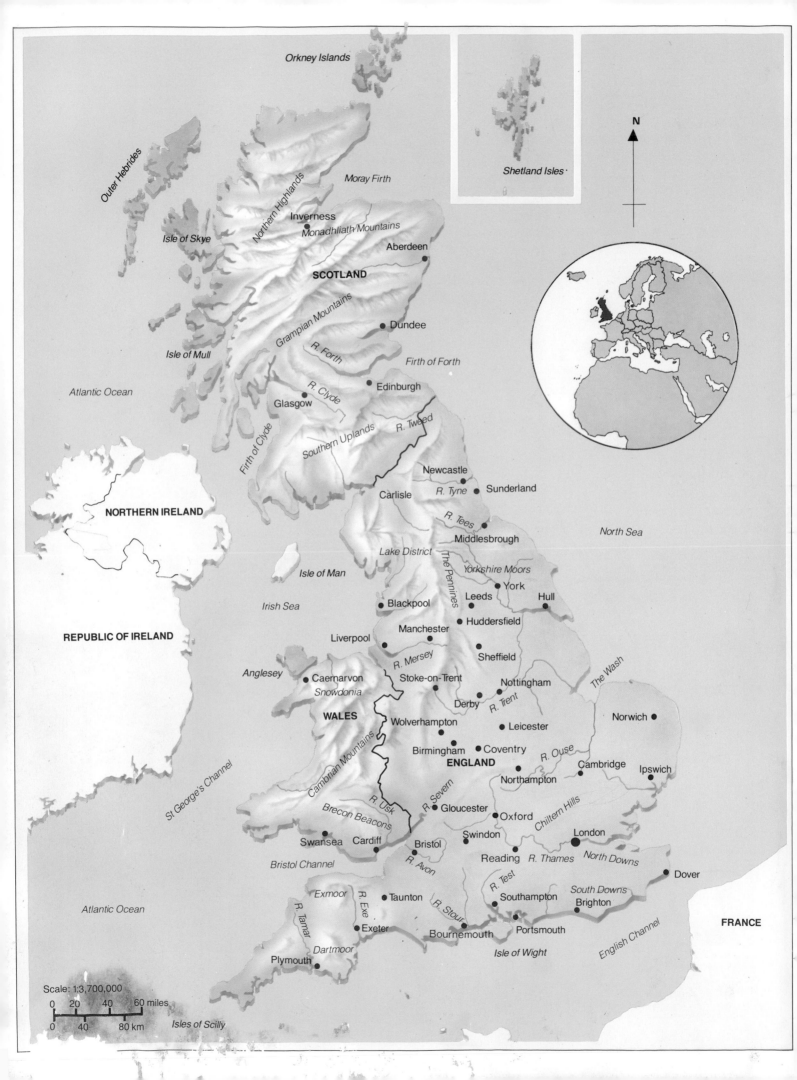

# Introduction

Britain can claim to be one of the world's most fascinating and influential countries. Each year huge numbers of visitors come to Britain to experience its unique traditions, history, scenery and way of life. For many it is a return to the land of their forefathers. People from Britain have settled in many different parts of the world, taking their culture and language with them.

Britain has undergone great changes in recent years. Peoples from many cultures have settled in Britain. Vast building schemes have changed the skylines of towns and cities. The people are gradually adapting to the new face of Britain.

As a small island Britain has always looked beyond its own shores. In the last century British trade, enterprise and industry brought about the creation of a great overseas empire. Today, Britain has a much reduced but still important role in world affairs as a member of the United Nations, the Commonwealth of Nations and the European Community. British enterprise and thought will, without doubt, continue to contribute much to commercial, cultural and scientific fields in the world today.

**Above:** A guardsman outside Windsor Castle, one of the Queen's homes, presents a traditional view of Britain.

**Below:** Dundee, one of Scotland's major cities, shows the mixture of old and new that is typical of Britain today.

# The land

Great Britain lies on the Atlantic coast of western Europe, separated from France by only 34 km (21 miles) of water. It is made up of three countries, England, Scotland and Wales. Great Britain with Northern Ireland forms the United Kingdom. The capital of the whole United Kingdom is London, in England. The capital of Wales is Cardiff (Caerdydd) and the Scottish capital is at Edinburgh.

Great Britain's largest island neighbour is Ireland. This is mainly occupied by the independent Republic of Ireland. The remainder is Northern Ireland which is a part of the United Kingdom. Many small islands are also linked with the United Kingdom. The Isle of Man and the Channel Islands have their own parliaments, but although they are administered by the British crown, they are not actually a part of the United Kingdom.

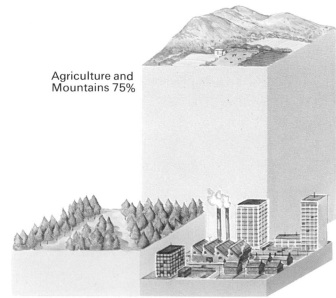

Agriculture and Mountains 75%

Forest 18%

Towns and Cities 7%

**Above:** Land use in Britain today. A large population is concentrated into a small land area amid open countryside.

**Below:** A typical English farmland scene with its patchwork of fields, hedgerows and scattered groups of trees.

Although a small island, Great Britain has a remarkable variety of landscapes. To the north and west are highlands – the mountains of Scotland, Cumbria and Wales, and the Pennine Chain. To the east are flat plains, and in the south are lowlands broken by low ranges of hills. To the southwest are the bleak moors of Devon and Cornwall.

The continent of Europe extends out below the waters of the Atlantic Ocean, in the form of a continental shelf. Great Britain is perched on this shelf, surrounded by the shallow waters of the North Sea, the Irish Sea and the English Channel.

A warm ocean current, the Gulf Stream, washes Britain's western shores. This water acts as an insulator, heating up and cooling down very slowly. Britain therefore enjoys warmer winters and cooler summers than other countries at the same latitude. The west of the island has a higher rainfall and slightly milder climate than the east.

**Above:** The Highlands of Scotland are Britain's least inhabited area. Loch Garry is in the Grampian mountain region.

**Below:** Rhossilli on the Gower Peninsula, South Wales. Wales is a land of rugged coastlines, valleys and mountains.

# The people

Who are the British? Like many nations, they are a complex mixture of different peoples. Many of them are descendants of the various invaders who have settled in the British Isles throughout history.

Among early arrivals were the Celts, a warlike people who overran western Europe sometime around 500 BC. Their descendants can be found today in Ireland, Scotland, the Isle of Man, Wales and Cornwall. Celtic languages include Irish and Scots Gaelic and Welsh, which is spoken by well over 500,000 people.

Southern Britain was occupied by Roman armies from AD 77–407. When they withdrew, the area now known as England was invaded by Germanic peoples from northern Europe: Angles, Saxons and Jutes, who became known as the English. The English language is now spoken throughout Britain. Later settlers included the Vikings and Danes from Scandinavia, and the Normans from France, who made the last successful invasion in 1066.

Romans
55 BC–400

Saxons
400–600

Picts/Scots
100–500

Jutes
400

Vikings
800–1000

Danes
800–1000

Normans
1066

**Above:** Settlements can be traced back to prehistoric times, but invasions brought most peoples to Britain.

**Below:** The British population today includes people of Caribbean, African and Asian ethnic backgrounds.

**Above:** Clive Whitby, a car factory foreman.

**Below:** Stanley Peacock is an insurance broker.

**Above:** Jane Beckley is a doctor.

**Below:** Peter Wood is a Welsh hill farmer.

Over the centuries many other peoples have come to Britain. The major cities of the United Kingdom have large Jewish and Irish communities, and often Greeks, Italians, Poles and Chinese as well. Since the 1950s many people have arrived from countries formerly ruled by Britain – from the Caribbean, from Africa, and from southeastern Asia.

The traditions of the people who live in Britain have been much enriched by such new influences. Today English children can be seen playing in Caribbean steel bands, and Bengali children may celebrate St David's Day in Welsh national costume.

To the rest of the world, the British sometimes present a rather perplexing picture. Traditionally, they have been seen as an insular people, rather reserved. The British have seen themselves as lovers of tradition, a moderate people, able to keep a "stiff upper lip" in a crisis. Is this picture still accurate? To some extent it is, but British society is undergoing great changes in all aspects of its life and culture.

**Above:** Stephen Pegler, a computer expert.

**Below:** Sylvia Cunningham runs a pub.

# Where people live

Great Britain is one of the world's most crowded countries. It has a population of more than 54 million, which means that there are on average more than 230 people to every square kilometre (more than 610 per square mile).

The vast majority of the population – more than 46 million – lives in England. Scotland, with 5 million, and Wales, with nearly 3 million, are more thinly populated. Both these countries contain large areas of moorland and mountains which have discouraged farming and made communications difficult.

Nearly half the people of Britain live in a band which runs diagonally from northwestern England to the southeast. This area takes in most of the major urban areas: Greater Manchester, Merseyside, South Yorkshire, Birmingham, West Midlands and Greater London. Other densely crowded areas in Britain include Clydeside, in the central lowlands of Scotland, and the southern coasts of England and Wales.

**Above:** Thixendale, in northern England, is one of the many villages which retain their traditional charm and serenity.

**Below:** Glasgow, the largest city in Scotland, is among the most overcrowded cities in Britain.

Left: Teignmouth, in southwestern England, is an old trading and fishing town. It has become a popular seaside resort and a home for many retired people.

Below: A typical surburban housing development near Henley-on-Thames in southern England.

Many of the huge cities grew up during the Industrial Revolution. They were built around coalfields, factories and textile mills. Today many of these industries have disappeared, and people are leaving the noisy road traffic and the poor quality, high-rent housing to move away to the suburbs. The building of new housing developments in the suburbs led to the decay of many inner-city areas.

Only 7 per cent of the total land area is taken up by cities, towns and suburbs – and yet over 90 per cent of the population lives in these urban areas. The reason is that there is little work to be found in the countryside. Modern farming makes use of machines rather than people, and one combine harvester replaces many workers.

As young people leave the countryside to look for work in the cities, many older people move to the countryside when they retire. In many parts of Britain this has completely changed the old patterns of village life.

# London

Beneath the tower blocks and pavements of modern London lie the ruins of temples and walls dating from the days of the Roman Empire. For nearly 2,000 years London has been the most important city in Britain. Its position on the River Thames made it into an international port and a centre for finance, trade, industry, arts and government.

Over the centuries London has spread over 15,850 sq km (6,120 sq miles) of the Thames valley, swallowing up towns and villages. The original site of London, now known as the City, contains many famous landmarks. The Tower of London, begun about 1079, was a former royal residence which later served as a prison. The Monument commemorates the fire in 1666 which consumed most of the old City. With the re-building came many famous churches, including St Paul's Cathedral. The City is now London's financial district – the home of the Stock Exchange, many banks and insurance companies.

**Above:** The ancient Tower of London is now dominated by the financial buildings of the City of London.

**Below:** Some of the major landmarks and sights which attract the 6 million visitors to London every year.

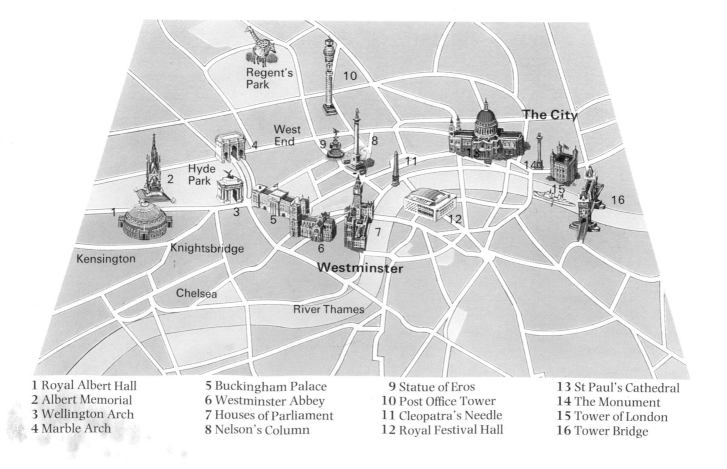

| | | | |
|---|---|---|---|
| 1 Royal Albert Hall | 5 Buckingham Palace | 9 Statue of Eros | 13 St Paul's Cathedral |
| 2 Albert Memorial | 6 Westminster Abbey | 10 Post Office Tower | 14 The Monument |
| 3 Wellington Arch | 7 Houses of Parliament | 11 Cleopatra's Needle | 15 Tower of London |
| 4 Marble Arch | 8 Nelson's Column | 12 Royal Festival Hall | 16 Tower Bridge |

West of the City is Westminster, which has gradually became the new heart of London. Here can be found Westminster Abbey, the Houses of Parliament and Buckingham Palace – the London home of the Queen. During the 19th century many new landmarks were built to commemorate famous events and people. Nelson's Column is a reminder of the famous naval victory at Trafalgar in 1805. Queen Victoria's husband, Albert, is honoured by a memorial and a concert hall. In recent times the Royal Festival Hall was built for the Festival of Britain in 1951 and the Post Office Tower has become a new symbol of London.

Piccadilly Circus, which features the famous statue of Eros, is in the West End with its large stores, art galleries, museums, theatres and restaurants. To the west is Knightsbridge, with its famous store Harrods, and other fashionable areas such as Kensington and Chelsea.

London is world-famous in many fields such as fashion and popular music. It is a city where old and new is found.

**Above:** This aerial view shows the major landmarks of Westminster, the West End and the beginnings of the City.

**Below:** London has many old customs and ceremonies. Here the Queen inspects soldiers at the "Trooping of the Colour".

# Fact file: land and population

## Key facts

**Location:** Off the northwest coast of the continent of Europe between latitudes 50°N and 60°N and longitudes 1°45′E and 8°10′E. Great Britain is Europe's largest island.

**Main parts:** Great Britain includes the countries of England, Scotland and Wales. Each country includes several islands, including the Isle of Wight (England); Anglesey (or Môn) (Wales); and the island groups of the Hebrides, Orkneys and Shetlands (Scotland).

**Area:** 229,979 sq km (88,795 sq miles). Of this total, England covers 130,439 sq km (50,363 sq miles); Scotland, 78,772 sq km (30,414 sq miles); and Wales, 20,768 sq km (8,018 sq miles).

**Population:** 54,773,000 (1982 estimate). Of this total, 46,799,000 live in England; 5,166,000 in Scotland; and 2,808,000 in Wales.

**Capital city:** London. (The capital of Scotland is Edinburgh and the capital of Wales is Cardiff.)

**Major cities** (England):
  London (6,765,000)
  Birmingham (1,017,000)
  Leeds (716,000)
  Sheffield (546,000)
  Liverpool (511,000)
  Bradford (465,000)
  Manchester (459,000)
  Bristol (400,000)
The leading Scottish cities are:
  Glasgow (762,000)
  Edinburgh (419,000)
  Aberdeen (190,000)
The leading Welsh cities are:
  Cardiff (280,000)
  Swansea (188,000)
  Newport (134,000)

**Main languages:** English (official); also Welsh, Scots, and many languages spoken by immigrants.

**Highest point:** Ben Nevis (Scotland), 1,343 m (4,406 ft)

**Longest rivers:**
Severn, 354 km (220 miles)
Thames, 346 km (215 miles)

**Largest lake:**
Loch Lomond, 70 sq km (27 sq miles)

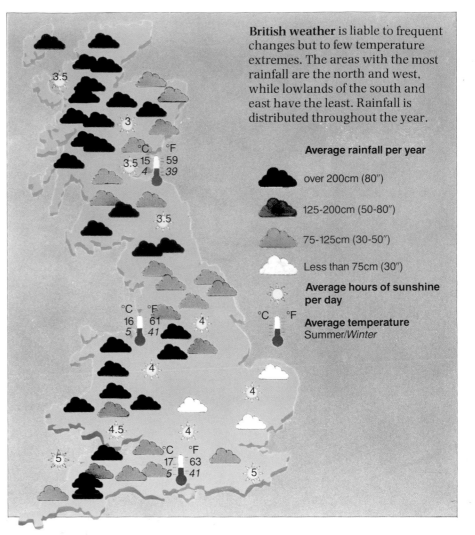

**British weather** is liable to frequent changes but to few temperature extremes. The areas with the most rainfall are the north and west, while lowlands of the south and east have the least. Rainfall is distributed throughout the year.

**Average rainfall per year**

over 200cm (80″)

125-200cm (50-80″)

75-125cm (30-50″)

Less than 75cm (30″)

**Average hours of sunshine per day**

**Average temperature**
Summer/*Winter*

USA            AUSTRALIA        FRANCE  GREAT BRITAIN

△ **A land area comparison**
Britain's land area of 229,979 sq km (88,759 sq miles) is small in comparison with many other countries. The U.S.A. has 9,370,000 sq km (3,600,000 sq miles), Australia, 7,650,000 sq km (2,470,000 sq miles) and France 547,026 sq km (211,208 sq miles). From the south coast of England to the extreme north it is just under 1,000 km (600 miles). Britain is just under 500 km (some 300 miles) across in the widest place. No place in Britain is more than 120 km (75 miles) from the sea.

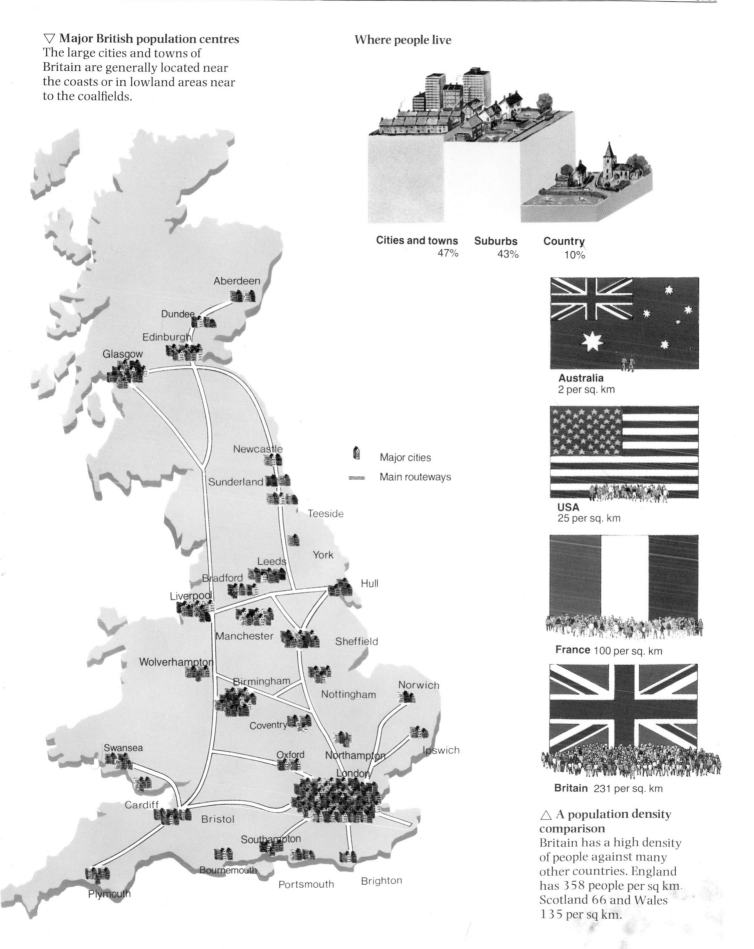

▽ **Major British population centres**
The large cities and towns of Britain are generally located near the coasts or in lowland areas near to the coalfields.

**Where people live**

**Cities and towns** 47%  **Suburbs** 43%  **Country** 10%

Aberdeen
Dundee
Edinburgh
Glasgow

Newcastle
Sunderland
Teeside
York
Leeds
Bradford
Liverpool
Hull
Manchester
Sheffield
Wolverhampton
Birmingham
Norwich
Nottingham
Coventry
Swansea
Oxford
Northampton
Ipswich
London
Cardiff
Bristol
Southampton
Bournemouth
Portsmouth
Brighton
Plymouth

🏢 Major cities
= Main routeways

**Australia**
2 per sq. km

**USA**
25 per sq. km

**France** 100 per sq. km

**Britain** 231 per sq. km

△ **A population density comparison**
Britain has a high density of people against many other countries. England has 358 people per sq km, Scotland 66 and Wales 135 per sq km.

# Home life

Most people in Britain aspire to have a house of their own with a garden. Today 80 per cent of the British people do live in houses rather than flats. Home ownership has become more possible and over 50 per cent today own their own home.

Nearly half of Britain's houses have been built since 1945. Slums and areas damaged by bombs in World War II have been replaced. Large modern housing developments have been built in country, town and suburban areas.

Living standards have also risen sharply since 1945. Almost every household today owns a refrigerator and a television; a large percentage now has a washing machine and a telephone. The majority also has central heating and at least one car.

Not everyone, however, enjoys a high standard of living. There is still sub-standard housing and a large number of homeless people. The rise in unemployment in the 1980's has forced many more people to depend on government benefits for financial support.

**Above:** Jill and Elliot Jefferies live in southwestern England. He is a civil servant and she works in a florist's shop.

**Below:** The family's living-room has simple modern furniture arranged around the television and hi-fi equipment.

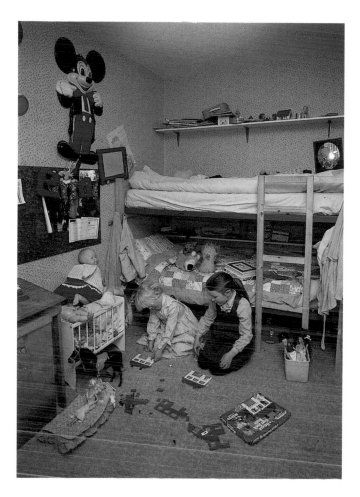

**Above:** A pet rabbit is kept in the back garden.

**Left:** The children share a bedroom which also serves as a playroom.

**Below:** The Jefferies family home is a typical three-bedroomed semi-detached house on a recently built development near Bath in southwestern England.

The size of each household has become smaller over the years. The average number has dropped from 4, at the beginning of the century, to only 2.7 today. Families are smaller, and elderly relatives now often live alone or in special homes, rather than remaining within the family circle.

The British are extraordinarily fond of animals. Half the households in Britain have a pet, whether it is a bird or a goldfish. There are nearly 5 million cats, and even more dogs, which remain the firm favourites.

As in many other countries, home life in Britain has changed a great deal in the age of television and video. Many people now prefer to stay at home for their entertainment. Cinema, dancing and pubs, however, remain popular with young people.

To make the home a more pleasant place in which to live, there has been an increased interest in home improvements, cooking and other home-orientated hobbies.

# Shops and shopping

Look down any of Britain's high streets and you will see the same names appearing. Shopping centres are dominated by a few giant chains of clothes shops, supermarkets and department stores.

Food shopping is becoming increasingly standardized. In 1971 there were 87,000 independent grocers; today there are only half that number. Most people buy their food in large supermarkets. In fact the two biggest supermarket chains account for an astonishing 31 per cent of all food sold.

The large companies succeed because they can buy their goods in bulk and thus offer goods at cheaper prices. They can advertise throughout the country and package their wares attractively. They can also afford the high rents charged for buildings in town centres. Small specialized shops are usually found away from the main streets. Prices are likely to be higher but the goods more individual.

**Above:** Supermarkets offer an increasing range of goods. Frozen foods have become very important as the majority of homes now have freezers.

**Below:** The main shopping centre in Liverpool has all the major British stores. Many cities have car-free areas to make shopping more pleasant.

Supermarkets are convenient and efficient, but many people feel that they lack the personal touch of the small corner shop. Family businesses, such as greengrocers, still prosper and today offer a wider choice of merchandise than ever before. The hustle and bustle of street markets, selling anything from fresh fish to antique silverware, always draw a large crowd.

Britain is famous for its clothes shops. For over twenty years London has led the world in fashion for young people. The tailors of London's Saville Row have long catered for more traditional tastes, with superb cloths and made-to-measure clothes.

Most British shops are open during the same hours, from 9:00 a.m. to 5:30 or 6:00 p.m. from Monday to Saturday. But many now stay open in the evening to suit those shoppers who are at work during the day, and Sunday opening is likely to become legal for all shops soon. Many small shops close for lunch. Most shops, apart from the large chain stores, close for a half-day on Wednesday or Thursday.

**Above:** Mohammed Hanif runs a grocery store. Many local shops in Britain are now run by Asian immigrants.

**Below:** A typical British shopping basket after a visit to the supermarket will contain a wide range of packaged goods.

# Cooking and eating

The British spend less of their incomes and time on food than many other nations. Their eating habits often reflect a far greater concern for convenience than for quality. Canned, frozen and packaged foods form a large part of the daily diet. Microwave ovens, which speed cooking time, have become very popular.

Breakfast used to be a very large meal, and even today some British families still sit down to a meal of cereal, eggs, bacon, sausages, mushrooms and tomatoes. However many people now prefer a lighter meal of cereal and toast with a cup of coffee or tea.

The main meal of the day is now usually eaten in the evening and many people only have a snack at lunchtime. A typical evening meal is a meat dish with vegetables, and a dessert. Beer and wine are becoming increasingly common at mealtimes. The chief meal of the week is still considered to be Sunday lunch. Roast beef, the traditional dish, is now expensive, and pork, chicken or lamb are more common.

**Above:** An average meal, generally served out in the kitchen, is easily and quickly prepared with a range of modern equipment.

**Right:** The family has a small dining room. Many families only eat together at the weekends.

The famous British afternoon tea, with its spread of cakes and sandwiches, is becoming increasingly rare except perhaps at weekends. Many young children, however, will have their last meal at about five o'clock.

Traditional British food is more often found in the home than in restaurants. Its wholesome and satisfying dishes are still well appreciated. England is famous for its game pies, roast beef and Yorkshire pudding, home-made Cornish pasties, milk puddings and cheeses. Welsh lamb is among the most tasty in the world, and haggis, made of sheep's liver, oatmeal and suet, is Scotland's national dish.

Many meals are eaten out. Pubs (public houses) are a part of the British tradition, being a combination of bar, social club and eating house. Take-away fast foods include the ever popular fish and chips, and, in recent years, American hamburgers. Restaurants serving French, Italian, Greek, Chinese or Indian food are found in almost every town.

**Above:** Almost every town in Britain has its fish and chip shop, serving one of the very first "takeaway" meals.

**Below:** Indian and Chinese restaurants are common in most British towns especially where there is a large ethnic community.

# Pastimes and sports

Most Britons now have more spare time than their grandparents could ever have imagined. The working week is usually between 35 and 40 hours spread over five days: working hours in 1900 were twice as long. The length of annual holidays has risen steadily as well, some workers receiving over five weeks per year. This increase in leisure time has stimulated traditional interests and produced many new activities.

The British are keen gardeners, and even those without a garden of their own often have a window box full of flowers, or rent a plot of land called an allotment on which to grow vegetables. Evening classes for adults are popular, with every interest catered for, from learning a language to yoga. National parks attract nature-lovers, horse and pony riders and ramblers. Fishing has more followers than any other sport.

**Above:** An allotment, can be a pleasant and rewarding pastime.
**Left:** River or sea fishing provides a very popular escape from the pressures of modern life.

**Below:** Football (soccer) is Britain's most popular sport. Many play the game at school and later play in local amateur sides. There are 130 professional clubs in Britain.

Never before have the British shown such an interest in staying fit and healthy. All over the country people run in marathon races and go jogging regularly. Both children and adults go on courses in order to learn how to hike, climb and canoe.

There are more than one thousand sports centres in the United Kingdom, and many of these are equipped with squash and tennis courts, gymnasiums and swimming pools. Most schools provide playing fields and sports facilities for their pupils.

The principal team games played were all invented in Britain: soccer, cricket, rugby union and rugby league. These are still hugely popular in Britain as games both to watch and play. Matches played against other countries provide great interest.

For many, sports provide an opportunity to gamble. Some 94 per cent of the adult population have gambled at some point in their lives, and 39 per cent admit to being regular gamblers. Dogs, horses and pigeons are raced for bets, and huge fortunes can be won on the football pools every week.

**Above:** A rugby union match between Wales and Scotland. Rugby union sides have 15 players. Rugby league, played mainly in northern England, has 13 players a side.

**Below:** Cricket is played by a huge number of village teams. English counties have professional teams. Cricketing nations such as Australia, the West Indies and Pakistan play the English national team.

# News and broadcasting

The small land area of Britain enables the various media, such as newspapers, magazines, radio and television, to reach almost every part of the country. On an average day nearly 3 out of 4 adults read one of the ten national papers. These range from the "quality" papers such as *The Times*, which has been in existence for over 200 years, to the brash "popular" papers such as *The Sun* and *The Daily Mirror*. All national newspapers are prepared in London's Fleet Street, the traditional home of the press. Outside London there are about 95 regional daily papers and some 950 weekly papers catering mainly for local news and interests.

The 5,000 periodicals published cover a huge range of subjects from general interests to academic topics. A strong book publishing industry produces nearly 50,000 titles each year. About one third of the population are members of the free public library service.

**Above:** A selection of national newspapers published on the same day provides very different approaches to news and opinions.

**Right:** Some of the many publications aimed at children and young people.
**Below:** Some of the many general magazines. *You* is issued with a Sunday newspaper.

**Above:** *TV Times* lists what is to be shown on commercial television. A typical day's viewing includes films, plays, current affairs, light entertainment, sport and politics.
**Right:** Nature documentaries are very popular.

Almost every home has access to television and radio. Watching television is a very popular leisure pastime in Britain. Two public bodies – the BBC (British Broadcasting Corporation) and the IBA (Independent Broadcasting Association) provide television and radio services. Both are obliged to provide a balance of subject matter, avoid bias and not offend good taste. The BBC, which provides two television channels, is financed by annual licence fees paid by every household having television. The IBA supervises 15 regional companies, who provide television programmes on the two commercial channels by showing advertisements. The BBC provides the four national radio channels, but local radio is operated by both the BBC and commercial stations.

Television viewing in recent years has been influenced by the rapid ownership of video recorders. Further changes are likely with the public growth of cable television stations and international broadcasting by satellites. Small computers have also been very readily accepted for entertainment and educational purposes.

**Above:** A scene from *Coronation Street*, the longest-running "soap opera".

**Below:** Terry Wogan, probably the most popular radio and television show presenter of the 1980s.

# Fact file: home life and leisure

## Key facts

**Population composition:** People under 16 years of age make up 22 per cent of the population; people between 16 and 64 make up 63 per cent; and people over 65 years make up 15 per cent.

**Average life expectancy at birth:** 74 years (1982), as compared with 72 years in 1970. In 1981 there were nearly 106 women to every 100 men. This is largely because women live longer than men.

**Rate of population increase:** 0.0 per cent per year in 1973–82, as compared with 0.6 per cent in 1960–70.

**Family life:** The average size of households is 2.7 people, as compared with 4 in 1900.

**Homes:** Owner-occupied houses numbered 12.2 million in 1981, almost three times as many as in 1951. Publicly rented homes increased from 2.5 million in 1951 to 6.8 million in 1981, but privately rented homes fell from 7.5 million in 1951 to 2.7 million in 1981.

**Work:** The average hours of work for both men and women in full-time employment in 1981 was 40.2 hours. The average weekly wage in 1984 was £159.30. The workforce in 1982 was 26.5 million, of whom 3,066,000 were unemployed.

**Prices:** Prices rose by 4 per cent per year in 1960–70 and by 14.2 per cent a year between 1970 and 1982. In 1984–5 it was 7 per cent.

**Religions:** In 1985 an estimated 16 per cent of the adult population were members of Christian churches. About 2 million were members of the Church of England, while the Church of Scotland had about 900,000 members. Other Protestant churches, include the Methodists (with nearly 500,000 adult members) and the Baptists (226,000 members). The Roman Catholic Church had over 2 million members. Members of other religions included about 900,000 Muslims, 111,000 Jews, 140,000 Hindus and 175,000 Sikhs.

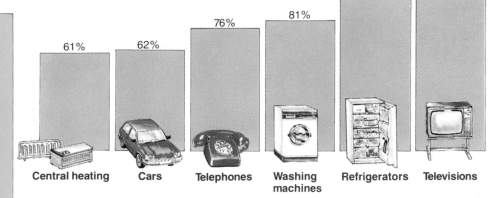

| Central heating | Cars | Telephones | Washing machines | Refrigerators | Televisions |
|---|---|---|---|---|---|
| 61% | 62% | 76% | 81% | 96% | 97% |

Fuel and power 5%

Clothing and footwear 7%

Household goods and services 7%

Entertainment and education 9%

Alcohol and tobacco 11%

Other goods and services 14%

Food 15%

Housing 15%

Transport and Communications 17%

△ **How many households owned goods in 1983**
Items being acquired more quickly than others in recent years are telephones, freezers and central-heating systems.

◁ **How the average household budget was spent in 1983**
This has shown significant changes in recent years. The proportion spent on food has fallen but spending on housing, alcohol, cars, televisions, telephones, other electrical goods, entertaining and overseas travel has risen.

▽ **British currency and postage stamps**
Britain adopted a decimal currency in 1971 – one pound (£) is divided into 100 pence (p). The coins now in circulation are 1p, 2p, 5p, 20p, 50p and £1.

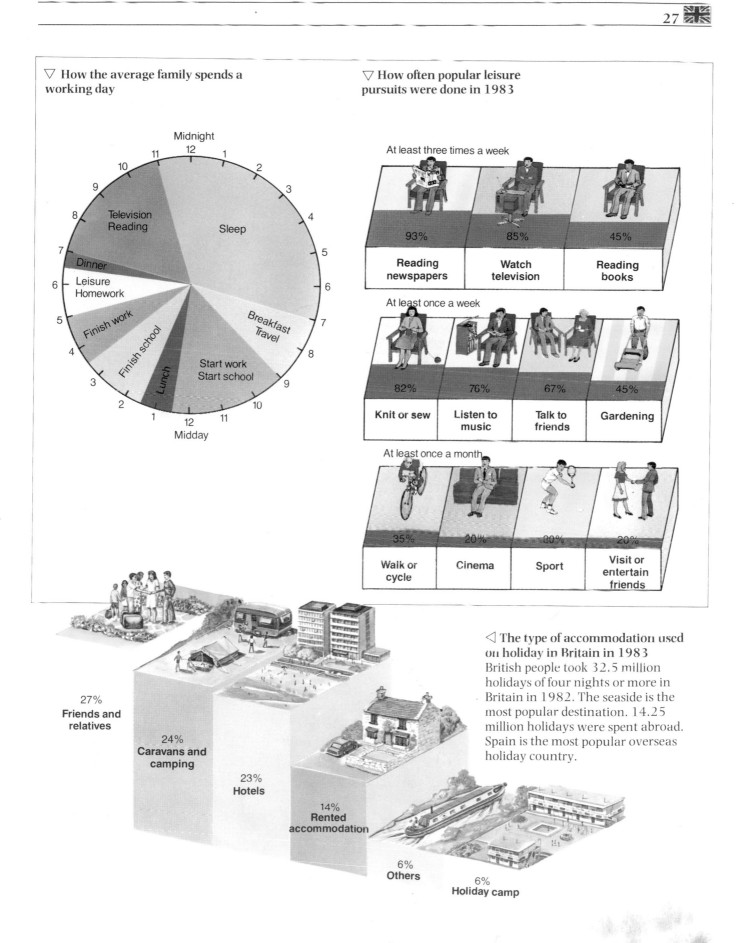

▽ How the average family spends a working day

▽ How often popular leisure pursuits were done in 1983

At least three times a week

93% Reading newspapers
85% Watch television
45% Reading books

At least once a week

82% Knit or sew
76% Listen to music
67% Talk to friends
45% Gardening

At least once a month

35% Walk or cycle
20% Cinema
20% Sport
20% Visit or entertain friends

27% Friends and relatives
24% Caravans and camping
23% Hotels
14% Rented accommodation
6% Others
6% Holiday camp

◁ The type of accommodation used on holiday in Britain in 1983
British people took 32.5 million holidays of four nights or more in Britain in 1982. The seaside is the most popular destination. 14.25 million holidays were spent abroad. Spain is the most popular overseas holiday country.

# Farming and fishing

Although less than 3 per cent of the working population works on the land, the farming industry produces almost two-thirds of Britain's food. Farming methods are very efficient with a high level of mechanization. Productivity per worker increased by over 160 per cent between 1962 and 1982 despite a drop in the numbers employed. About 75 per cent of Britain's land area is devoted to farming.

Most of the arable crops, such as cereals and vegetables, are grown in eastern and central southern parts of England and eastern Scotland, where the land is flat. Dairy farming is found mainly in the western half of Britain, where a higher rainfall produces lusher grass. The majority of beef cattle and sheep are reared on the hill and upland areas of Scotland, Wales, and northern and southwestern England. Many breeds of British cattle, sheep and pigs have been exported to countries around the world. Britain is also a major exporter of agricultural produce, machinery, fertilizers and food products.

**Above:** Most livestock is bought and sold by auction at weekly markets. Competition is fierce for the best animals.

**Below:** Britain has some 57,500 combine harvesters and over half a million tractors used by a workforce of 600,000.

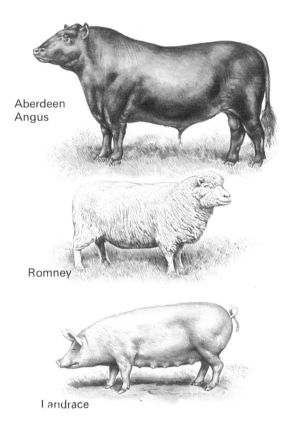

Aberdeen
Angus

Romney

Landrace

**Above:** A selection of British agricultural products.

**Left:** Some famous breeds.

**Below:** Fish being unloaded on the quayside at Polperro, in the extreme southwest of England.

Britain plays a leading role in research into new crops, pesticides and farming methods.

The work of both government and private research institutions have had important effects on British and international agriculture.

In recent years there has been concern about the environmental effects of modern farming methods. To make larger fields, hedges have been torn out and wildlife displaced. Animal rights groups are protesting about the keeping of animals, such as pigs and poultry, in conditions where they are deprived of sunlight, fresh air and exercise.

Fishing is an important industry which supplies nearly 70 per cent of home needs. Inshore boats from major ports such as Aberdeen, Grimsby, Hull and Yarmouth land most of the catch, which includes cod, haddock, mackerel and plaice. Strict limits are put on sizes of catches to prevent over-fishing. Fish farming is expanding, with salmon, trout and shellfish being the major products.

# Natural resources and industry

Britain has the largest energy resources of any country in Western Europe. The rise of Britain as a great industrial power was largely based on coal, which remains the richest natural source with reserves for at least 300 years. Underground mining is most common. The coal industry, which came under public ownership in 1947, has been much reduced in size during this century due to the use of other fuels. Over one-third of energy is still generated from coal, and new investment schemes are being introduced to exploit new pits and increase productivity.

Until 1975 Britain imported almost all of its oil needs. The discovery of oil under the North Sea has made Britain self-sufficient and the world's fifth largest oil producer. Natural gas, also found under the North Sea, has become a very important energy source. Despite concern about its dangers, nuclear power is being steadily developed as a long-term source of electricity.

Britain is not rich in many other minerals and has to import most of its needs.

**Above:** Oil and gas were discovered in the North Sea in 1969. Huge advances have been made in undersea exploration and in the development of equipment. In 1985, there were 24 off-shore crude oil fields and 6 major gas fields.

**Left:** Coal mining has been made safer and more efficient by the use of modern machinery such as this giant cutter. Britain is a world leader in advanced coal-mining technology.

**Above:** The symbols of some of Britain's leading car manufacturers.

**Right:** A robot production line at British Leyland.

**Below:** Tartan cloth being woven in Scotland.

The traditional economic strength of Britain was based on manufacturing industries supplied by the rich coalfields and iron ore deposits. Iron and steel, textiles, heavy machinery, ship-building and later motor vehicles were the mainstay of British wealth and employment. Today most of these industries have fallen into decline owing mainly to the stiff competition from other nations. The surviving parts of these industries now concentrate on manufacture for the home market and high-quality products for export. A ready market abroad is found for firms such as Rolls-Royce, Jaguar and Rover, as well as British wool products.

In 1984, four of the top 20 industrial companies in Europe were British. British Petroleum is Europe's largest company. The largest British manufacturing companies are British American Tobacco and Imperial Chemical Industries.

# Trade with the world

Overseas trade has always been Britain's life-blood. Despite the decline in the traditional industries, Britain is the world's fifth largest trading nation and part of the world's largest trading area, the European Economic Community. Britain exports about 30 per cent of its total output of goods and services. Many British industries have undergone great changes to improve their position in world trade, especially in aerospace, chemicals, scientific instruments, oil and electronics. Britain was a pioneer in computers and has one of the largest computer industries outside the United States. The use of robots in industry is increasing rapidly, particularly in car manufacturing. The chemical industry is large enough to make Britain one of the top four chemical-producing nations of the world. Aerospace production has made great progress in recent years with the United States as its major market for civil and military aircraft, engines and equipment. The United States is Britain's largest single market, taking 13.4 per cent of exports in 1982.

**Above:** Britain is in the forefront of developing new technology. These workers are testing integrated circuits.

**Below:** Britain's newest airliner, the BAe 146, in production at the British Aerospace factory in southern England.

![The London Stock Exchange trading floor]

Britain makes very substantial earnings out of a wide range of services to other nations. This "invisible" trade includes insurance, banking, technical and scientific expertise and tourism. The City of London has the greatest concentration of banks in the world, the world's largest insurance market, a major Stock Exchange and the world-wide sale of many important commodities. Britain is a leader in the provision of software and computer services. Software development in Britain has contributed to the development of computer application in many countries. The British film and television industry has gained a notable reputation. Television programmes are exported to many countries of the world. Many foreign-financed films are made in British studios using specialized cinematic techniques. The British tourist industry has grown rapidly, and the annual 12 million visitors provide substantial foreign earnings.

**Above:** The London Stock Exchange is the focus of British financial dealing and has world-wide influence.

**Below:** *Superman* is just one of the many major films made with American finance at Pinewood Studios near London.

# Transportation

A key to Britain's industrial growth was the development of good transportation systems. In the 18th century a network of canals was built, and in the 19th century Britain pioneered the use of railways. The 20th century saw the growth of air and road travel. Britain now has a very comprehensive transportation network covering the country.

Roads are the most important means of transportation, both for goods and for people. There are nearly 20 million vehicles on Britain's roads, of which three-quarters are cars. More than 82 per cent of all freight is carried by road. Motorways link major cities and industrial areas, but traffic jams and pollution from exhaust fumes still create problems in the towns.

The railway system provides a fast and safe inter-city link for passengers and freight. Many lines are electrified and modern diesel engines can average speeds of 200 km/h (125 mph) on long journeys.

**Below:** Paddington Station in London, from where high-speed diesel trains take passengers to South Wales and the West of England.

**Above:** Since Britain's first motorway was built in 1957, a motorway network has been constructed throughout Britain.

**Above:** Symbols of the major transportation systems. From top to bottom: British Railways; British Airways; the National Bus Company, which operates a network of local and long-distance services.

About 26 million passengers and 427 million tonnes of freight pass through the 300 British seaports every year. Many goods are now packed in standard containers so that they can be lifted directly from lorries or trains into the cargo hold of a ship.

The British merchant navy fleet in 1983 was the sixth largest in the world. The fleet is one of the safest in the world due, in part, to the excellent search and rescue services operating around the coasts of Britain. The Coastguard Service is aided by the 250 stations of the Royal National Lifeboat Institution.

London's Heathrow Airport carries more international traffic than any other in the world. Gatwick, London's second major airport, is the world's fifth busiest international airport. Other leading airports are at Manchester, Glasgow, Luton, Aberdeen, Birmingham, Belfast and Edinburgh. British Airways is one of the world's leading airlines and in terms of international passengers carried, it is the largest. The airline flies to 60 countries.

**Above:** The port of Dover in southeast England handles large quantities of passengers and freight with Europe. Many ports have been modernized to cope with container ships.

**Below:** This driver of a long distance bus takes passengers from London to Glasgow in under eight hours. Such services offer cheaper but slower travel than by rail.

# Fact file: economy and trade

## Key facts

**Structure of production:** Of the total GDP (the value of all economic activity in the UK), farming, forestry and fishing contribute 2 per cent, industry 33 per cent and services 65 per cent.

**Farming:** Britain imports food, although it produces enough of some products, such as eggs, milk and wheat, to meet home demands. *Chief crops:* barley, oats, oilseed rape, potatoes, sugar beet, vegetables, wheat. *Livestock (UK):* cattle, 13,242,000; sheep, 33,053,000; pigs, 8,023,000; poultry, 135,363,000.

**Forestry and fishing:** Forests cover 7 per cent of England, 12 per cent of Scotland and 11 per cent of Wales. Britain's fishing fleet has 6,600 inshore and 239 deep-sea vessels.

**Mining:** Of the total value of minerals produced in 1982, oil accounted for 65 per cent, coal 24 per cent and natural gas 5 per cent. Britain imports many metals.

**Energy:** In 1982, of the total primary energy production, coal supplied 36.2 per cent, oil 35.6 per cent, natural gas 23 per cent, nuclear energy 5.1 per cent, and hydroelectric power 0.8 per cent.

**Manufacturing:** Major industries include engineering (including vehicles, engines and other equipment), electrical goods, chemicals, textiles and construction.

**Transportation** (UK 1982): *Roads:* 366,545 km (227,767 miles), including 2,675 km (1,662 miles) of motorway; *Rail:* 17,230 km (10,706 miles) of track; *Waterways:* about 4,000 km (2,486 miles) of canals and river navigation.

**Trade** (UK 1982): *Total imports:* US $100,882 million; *exports:* US $105,588 million. The UK is the world's fifth most important trading nation.

**Economic growth:** The average growth rate of the UK's gross national product (1973–82) was 0.9 per cent per year. In 1983 it was 3.25 per cent.

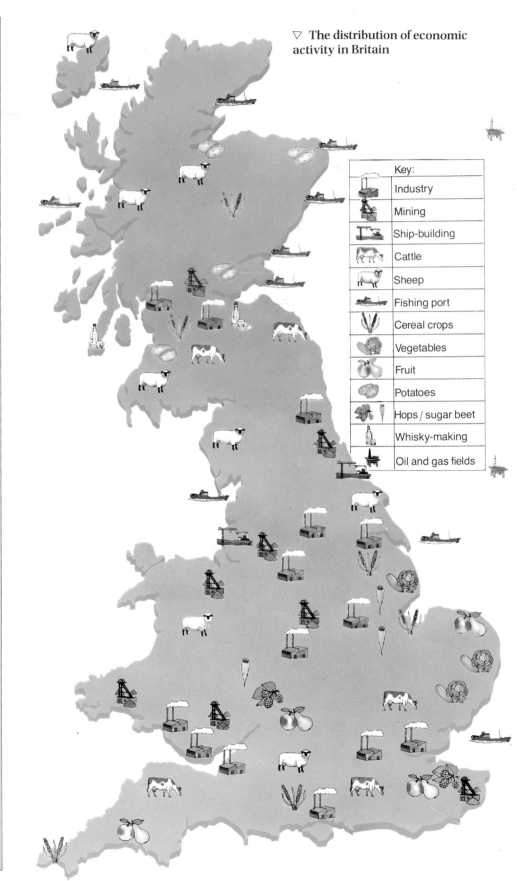

▽ **The distribution of economic activity in Britain**

| Key: | |
|---|---|
| | Industry |
| | Mining |
| | Ship-building |
| | Cattle |
| | Sheep |
| | Fishing port |
| | Cereal crops |
| | Vegetables |
| | Fruit |
| | Potatoes |
| | Hops / sugar beet |
| | Whisky-making |
| | Oil and gas fields |

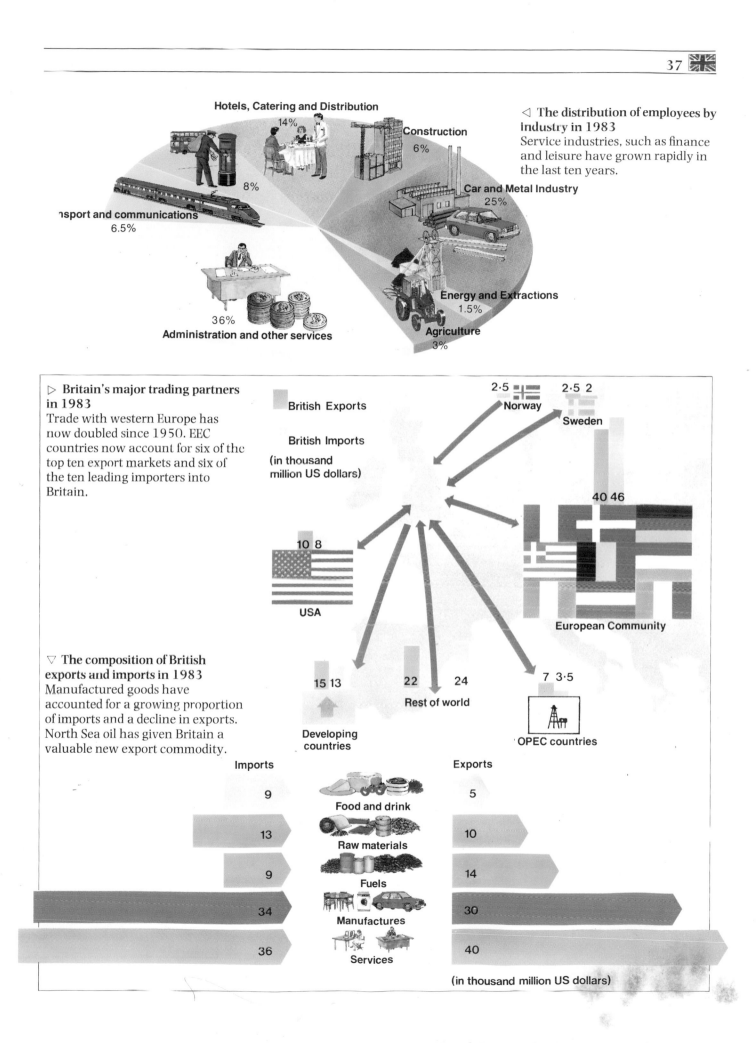

**Hotels, Catering and Distribution**
14%

**Construction**
6%

**Car and Metal Industry**
25%

8%

◁ **The distribution of employees by industry in 1983**
Service industries, such as finance and leisure have grown rapidly in the last ten years.

nsport and communications
6.5%

**Energy and Extractions**
1.5%

**Agriculture**
3%

36%
**Administration and other services**

▷ **Britain's major trading partners in 1983**
Trade with western Europe has now doubled since 1950. EEC countries now account for six of the top ten export markets and six of the ten leading importers into Britain.

**British Exports**

**British Imports**

(in thousand million US dollars)

2·5 **Norway**

2·5 2 **Sweden**

40 46

10 8
**USA**

**European Community**

▽ **The composition of British exports and imports in 1983**
Manufactured goods have accounted for a growing proportion of imports and a decline in exports. North Sea oil has given Britain a valuable new export commodity.

15 13
**Developing countries**

22 24
**Rest of world**

7 3·5
**OPEC countries**

**Imports**

**Exports**

9 — **Food and drink** — 5

13 — **Raw materials** — 10

9 — **Fuels** — 14

34 — **Manufactures** — 30

36 — **Services** — 40

(in thousand million US dollars)

# Education

British children between the ages of 5 and 16 are required by law to receive full-time education. Some go on to study in the sixth form (the final stage at school) until age 18.

Since 1944, free education has been available to all. Over 10 million pupils attend 35,000 primary and secondary schools, most of which are run by local education authorities. They charge no fees for teaching, books or equipment. The money for these comes from rates and taxes.

Many children go to a nursery school before starting at a primary school, but, at present, the facilities are usually inadequate to meet the demand for places. About half of four-year olds now receive nursery education.

Primary education, beginning at age 5, is made up of two stages, infant and junior. Basic skills such as reading, writing and numbers, as well as a wide range of general subjects, are taught in an informal atmosphere with no standard curriculum.

**Above:** Yvonne Keeler, a primary school teacher in London. She teaches a class of 30 children of many different ethnic backgrounds.

**Below:** Most schools have a range of equipment to assist learning. The class here is learning about the operations and uses of computers.

**Above:** Most pupils in secondary school learn at least one modern language.

**Left:** School boys at Eton, a major public school.

**Below:** Pupils sitting for secondary school examinations. Examination success is needed for many jobs and is essential for further education.

Secondary schooling starts at the age of 11. Here children start more advanced subjects, such as foreign languages and science. Most secondary schools are organized on "comprehensive" lines. These schools accept all the children from one area, regardless of their abilities, and educate them together.

Private education is still available in Britain. More than 2,500 schools still charge for their services. Many pupils are boarders who live at the school. Private pupils first go to a preparatory school, from ages 7–13, and then to what is known (confusingly) as a public school.

More than a third of young people receive some form of education after leaving school. About 300,000 attend the 33 universities in England, the 8 in Scotland and the University of Wales. Grants are available to students to pay fees and living expenses. The "Open University" provides instruction for home-based students through television broadcasts and correspondence with tutors.

# The arts

Britain's chief contribution to world culture has been its literature. The English language has proved to be an ideal medium for poets, playwrights and novelists.

A great flowering of popular dramatic art occurred in England some four centuries ago. William Shakespeare (1564–1616) stands supreme, but his contemporaries included other men of genius, such as Christopher Marlowe (1564–93) and Ben Jonson (1572–1637).

Britain is famous for its poetry. Scotland's national poet is Robert Burns (1759–96). William Wordsworth (1770–1850) was one of several English Romantic poets, who were inspired by nature and by the ideals of liberty expressed in the French Revolution. The others include Percy Bysshe Shelley (1792–1822), Lord Byron (1788–1824) and John Keats (1795–1821) who wrote superb poetry that is still much read and appreciated today.

**Above:** William Shakespeare, one of the world's greatest literary geniuses, was born in England, at Stratford-on-Avon.

**Right:** Charles Dickens, the chronicler of Victorian Britain.
**Below:** Robert Burns, Scotland's greatest poet, is still revered.

The English novel reached its peak in the 19th century, in the works of William Makepeace Thackeray (1811–63), Charlotte Brontë (1816–55), George Eliot (1819–80) and Thomas Hardy (1840–1928). Few writers succeeded in capturing the spirit of their age more than Charles Dickens (1812–70). In the 20th century the tradition has been continued with several great observers of human nature including D. H. Lawrence (1885–1930) and Virginia Woolf (1882–1941).

In the visual arts, Britain has produced individuals of genius rather than famous schools of painting. William Blake (1757–1827) and Joseph Turner (1775–1851) are two examples. Few artists have interpreted the British landscape as subtly as John Constable (1776–1837). In the 20th century the paintings of Francis Bacon and David Hockney are much admired. British sculpture has also achieved world renown through the work of Henry Moore.

Britain today remains a world centre for the arts, literature, music and drama.

**Above:** *The Shipwreck,* painted by J. M. W. Turner, shows a superb mastery of the effects of light.

**Below:** The Tate Gallery in London has a world-famous art collection. Britain has a large number of art galleries and museums.

# The making of modern Britain

In 1800 the population of Britain was about 10.5 million. By 1901 it was 38.2 million, and growing. Chief reasons for this explosion were improvements in medical care and nutrition: people lived longer and fewer children died.

Britain was the world's first industrialized country. Before the 18th century most people had lived by farming. But then new processes were invented for weaving cloth and forging iron, and a network of canals and railways was built. Poor people flooded into new factory towns, such as Manchester, to find work.

While the factory owners grew rich, the workers endured appalling hardship and poverty and squalid housing conditions. This was the world portrayed so vividly by such authors as Charles Dickens.

The expansion of the British Empire during the 19th century provided cheap raw materials which British factories processed and exported around the world. Enterprise and trade were largely responsible for the creation of the world's largest empire.

**Above:** Coalbrookdale, near Shrewsbury, seen here in 1758, was one of the early industrial towns in England.

**Below:** Queen Victoria, during whose long reign (1837–1901) Britain reached the peak of its wealth and power.

Britain was the most powerful country in the world during most of the 19th century. Its huge navy really did "rule the waves". From the Crimean War (against Russia, 1854–56) until the Boer War (against South Africans of Dutch descent 1899–1902) British troops extended and defended the Empire in many distant parts of the world.

In 1914 Great Britain, faced with the growing might of Germany, became involved in a disastrous war which lasted four long years. Over a million British troops were killed in the brutal slaughter of World War I. The war left a legacy of bitterness among both victors and defeated. British soldiers had been told they were fighting for "a land fit for heroes". What many returned to was poverty and unemployment.

The rise of fascism in Germany and Italy resulted in World War II, 1939–1945, in which Britain was among the victorious nations, but at a great cost. In the post-war world Britain had to struggle to find a new role among larger and better equipped nations.

**Above:** Britain lost three-quarters of a million men in the brutal trench warfare of World War I. **Left:** British troops escape from France in 1940.

**Below:** Winston Churchill joins the crowds celebrating Victory in Europe day after the surrender of Germany in May 1945.

# Britain in the modern world

In the twenty years after World War II, the majority of British people experienced a steady growth in living standards and material wealth. A "welfare state", created by a socialist government in 1947, provided almost free medical treatment, unemployment pay and many other social security benefits. Vast house-building schemes gave many people new homes with modern facilities.

This apparent well-being, however, masked great weaknesses in the British economy. In the late 1960s and 1970s inflation and loss of competitiveness in overseas markets led to a steady growth in unemployment, particularly in the traditional industries.

The Conservative government of Margaret Thatcher, first elected in 1979, pledged to reduce inflation, restore the competitiveness of British industry and cut government spending. By 1985 the government appeared to be making progress toward economic health. Inflation was down to 5% in 1984 but unemployment was at a record level of 3 million.

**Above:** Prime Minister Edward Heath commits Britain to Europe in 1973. This act was delayed for several years by opposition from within Britain and a veto by France.

**Below:** Striking coal miners face police in 1984 during the year-long dispute over job losses. Successive governments have clashed with the trade union movement over economic policies.

British society has also undergone great changes. Women have claimed a much broader role and now comprise about 40% of the working population. Efforts have also been made to improve the position in society of various ethnic minorities, particularly those of Asian and Caribbean origin.

Britain has had to adapt to a changed role in the world since the granting of independence to the colonies. Through the Commonwealth of Nations, with the Queen at its head, Britain's links with them are still maintained. The entry of Britain into the European Community in 1973 further established Britain's new role as a European, rather than a world power.

Britain's defence policy is based on the North Atlantic Treaty Organization (NATO) and plays a full part in the provision of troops and weapons. British troops also form part of UN peace-keeping forces in many of the world's trouble spots.

Britain now stands at a crossroads in its history. It faces many future problems: how to further modernize its industry and make full use of its facility for innovation; how to best care for the environment; how to maintain a fair and just society and how to secure peace, at home and abroad.

**Above left:** Women demonstrate about the basing of American nuclear missiles in Britain.
**Above:** Prime Minister Margaret Thatcher reaches an agreement, in 1984, for the colony of Hong Kong to be returned to China in 1997.

**Below:** The wedding of Prince Charles to Lady Diana Spencer, in 1981, further enhanced the popularity of the Monarchy. For over 30 years the Queen has maintained the respect and affection of the British people.

# Fact file: government and world role

## Key facts

**Official name:** The United Kingdom of Great Britain and Northern Ireland.

**Flag:** Union Flag, known as the Union Jack.

**National anthem:** *God Save the Queen.*

**National government:** *Head of State:* the Monarch. Elizabeth II (born 1926) became Queen in 1952 on the death of her father George VI. *Legislature:* Parliament (which passes laws, votes for taxation to carry on the government's work and examines the government's policies and administration) consists of the Monarch, the House of Lords and the House of Commons with 650 elected members. The Prime Minister (usually leader of the majority party in the Commons) selects a Cabinet of ministers to govern the nation.

**Local government:** England is divided into 7 metropolitan counties and 39 non-metropolitan counties, although plans were announced in 1985 to abolish the metropolitan counties. Wales has 8 counties and Scotland 9 regions and 3 Island Authorities.

**Armed forces** (1983): *Army:* The Regular Army contained 152,900 men and 6,100 women. *Navy:* The Royal Navy consisted of 60,100 men and 3,900 women. *Air Force:* The Royal Air Force contained 84,500 men and 5,400 women.

**Economic Alliances:** Since January 1, 1973, Britain has been a member of the European Economic Community (or Common Market). Britain also belongs to the Organization for Economic Co-operation and Development (OECD).

**Political Alliances:** Britain is a member of the UN, the Council of Europe and the western defence alliance, the North Atlantic Treaty Organization (NATO). It is also a member of the Commonwealth, an association of 49 independent nations. Britain is also a member of the Colombo Plan to promote development in Asia and the Pacific.

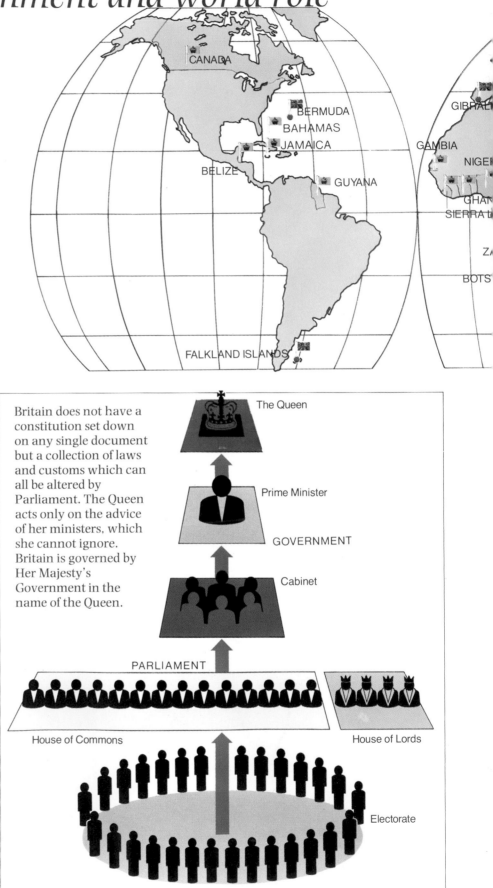

CANADA
BERMUDA
BAHAMAS
JAMAICA
BELIZE
GUYANA
FALKLAND ISLANDS

GIBRAL
GAMBIA
NIGE
GHA
SIERRA L
Z
BOTS

Britain does not have a constitution set down on any single document but a collection of laws and customs which can all be altered by Parliament. The Queen acts only on the advice of her ministers, which she cannot ignore. Britain is governed by Her Majesty's Government in the name of the Queen.

The Queen

Prime Minister

GOVERNMENT

Cabinet

PARLIAMENT

House of Commons

House of Lords

Electorate

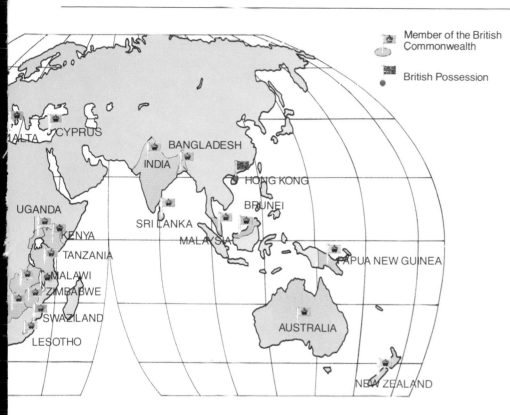

Member of the British Commonwealth

British Possession

◁ **Major overseas possessions**
Britain has 15 remaining dependent territories in various parts of the world. Their combined population is 5.5 million of which 5.3 million live in Hong Kong.

◁ **Major countries of the Commonwealth of Nations**
The Queen is recognized as Head of the Commonwealth and is also Head of State in 18 of the 49 countries.

Australia 10,780

Belgium 9,160

Canada 12,000

France 10,390

West Germany 11,420

Italy 6,350

Japan 10,100

Netherlands 9,910

New Zealand 7,410

Spain 4,800

United Kingdom 9,050

USA 14,090

(In US dollars)

△ **National wealth created per person in 1983**
Britain has fallen behind most other industrial nations. It remains to be seen whether Britain can work its way towards full economic health and have living standards equal to those of other developed nations.

▽ **The countries of the EEC**
The aims of the Community are to bring a closer union between the peoples of Europe and to provide economic expansion. Many trade barriers have been abolished between member countries, workers can move freely and there are common policies for agriculture and fisheries. Community decisions are taken by a Council of Ministers. A European Parliament, first elected in 1979, debates all policy issues put forward by the Council. Britain has 81 of Parliament's 434 members.

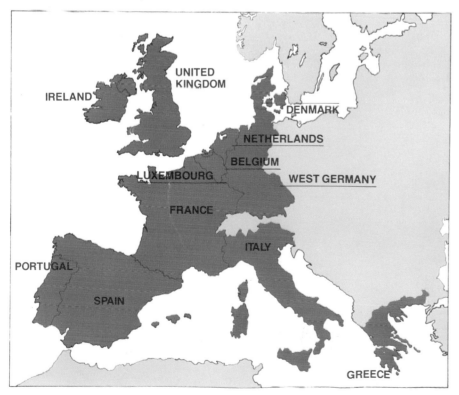

# Index

PRINTED IN BELGIUM BY
proost
INTERNATIONAL BOOK PRODUCTION